Animals

Pooja Hiremath

BookLeaf Publishing

Presentation by *BookLeaf Publishing*

Web: www.bookleafpub.com

E-mail: info@bookleafpub.com

ISBN: 9789395271110

First edition 2022

DEDICATION

To the walls of Demarest, and all the stories they could tell...

ACKNOWLEDGEMENT

Thank you to those who stuck around.
You know who you are.

once upon a time

an only child, I was very lonely
mint chocolate chip dress and sneakers, I stuck
out
against the ragtag group of smiles speckled with
mud
from playing tug-of-war in damp grass.
sheltered and shy, I tried to camouflage into the
oak
I leaned on watching them, wondering
what it would be like to have a bigger family.
international Poodle waved
western Bengal lifted a cup of tea to me
lithe Swan danced over and took my arm
distant Wolf stood on the frays of the group
musical Elephant invited me to play the bongos
ruffled Cub caught my eye, "come eat with us!"
I accepted the offer, trusting our pact would be
solid.

intoxicated by shared mirth
I sought to belong in the squad
Elephant coaxed me to come out to his room.
"there's blue cotton candy!"
instead I found Bengal sipping Bombay
Sapphire

Wolf and Cub playing Edward Fortyhands on
the floor.
Cub chugged to win. when he spilled
on himself in the process, I smirked.
Wolf stopped the game.
aloof, he stood and brushed past me.
"It's too crowded in here."
seeing me taken aback, Bengal jumped in.
"don't mind him."
Poodle and Swan walked in, hooked their arms
through mine.
"night's young, let's prowl!"
I giggled at Swan's eagerness.
the boys followed us out of the room. we walked
into
a plume of smoke. "why not go outside?" I
asked.
Wolf flicked my shoulder.
"bites from - what are they? bees? killer bees."
I laughed. "you mean mosquitoes?"
he insisted and I continued to laugh,
once again taken aback
at the change in his demeanor.
the girls tugged my arms, and I stumbled
forward
an extra look over my shoulder at Wolf.
he smirked back
falling in step

behind Elephant and Bengal, Cub flanking his side.

lighter

we lounged in the second floor rec room
Swan and Poodle painting nails
Elephant scrolling through his phone
Bengal giving Cub IT tips
as I munched on my fat sandwich.
Wolf flicked his smoking cig
at the trash can next to me
it hit my shoulder
I cringed at the sting
igniting a chorus of distaste toward Wolf.
Bengal, ready with his first aid
nursed my wound -
Wolf had already moved on
flicking his next cig out the window
careless about contact
paper, rock, dry or wet
his heat his defense.

baker girl

in a cloud of nutmeg and vanilla
I was inspired to put in a
dash of butterscotch then
lather on chocolate frosting
the basic ingredient for disaster
cooking a birthday treat for a picky wolf
to soften him up
one cake was not enough
red velvet cupcakes, brownies, cookies
impression ruined: Wolf didn't like sweet things
how little I knew him
while Cub indulged in his snacks.

this won't matter in five years

6

mellowed, he showed appreciation of my effort
to please him by roaming his hands on me
and leaving a trail of fireworks in my mind.
we squeezed together on the twin cot
like our lives depended on the raft
flushed, I wanted more
"what will this mean tomorrow?"
flushed, Wolf wanted sleep
"depends on my dreams"
when I awoke
I was alone.

adventures

part one: after show
I couldn't fall back asleep
so I ventured into the basement
entranced by the Cloud Atlas tune
he was a flurry of piano keys
a symphony that ended in haste
when Wolf appeared and
jerked his head to the door
I asked for an encore but
Cub shied away from the commendation.

part two: miles away
debate team traveler, Bengal
slept on a wayward couch
waiting to catch his bus
I covered him with a spare blanket
he woke startled by kindness. "why?"
"if it were me -"
"do you want to come with me?"
I snuck aboard with Bengal
no plans, but we had melody
rocking shoulder to shoulder
pretending we were walking on the moon
watching autumn leaves cascade around us
I dozed off and Bengal lent me

his jacket for cover.

straying

Cub asked me if I was ready
for a night of bonfire and Bacardi
"of course."
a brush through my mane, with a polished coat
ready to lope after the usual crew
Swan and I skipped ahead of Poodle
Cub and Wolf slinked together in the rear
with furtive whispers

Bengal was busy stoking the fire, but
he asked me to save the last dance.
I saw Wolf mingle with colliding bodies,
Swan disappeared with Elephant,
Cub asked me to retrieve him kindling
agreeing, he called me his kitten
I balked, I belonged to no one.
picking up a stray branch, I threw it at him
Cub's attention on the red cup in Poodle's hand.

swaying by myself, a hand slipped around my
waist
I leaned back into familiarity
Wolf tugged me into isolation
an empty parking lot with dandelions
to pull me down but I stopped

"not this way."
snubbed, Wolf deftly moved on
claiming Poodle as his prize.

tipping point

his ease of unfaithfulness
should have been expected
but fractured my rationality nevertheless
I picked up his neglected tweed coat
plucked the quarters from its pockets
to buy closure -
I wasn't Wolf's keeper.
I handed the remainder to Cub
joining Swan to carry a dizzy Poodle home
catching Bengal's concerned eye -
I don't know what I want anymore.

retribution

accusation waited me.
Wolf found me stargazing, Cub in tow
to ask for the missing pocket contents
in reply to snarls, I parried back evenly
our prides scraping like sandpaper
neither of us backing down
from our baleful glare.
disgusted by his silent participation,
Cub turned away -
I surrendered. For him, I told the truth
but his disappointment sweltered
the chit with her name and ten digits
handed to Wolf, for a notion we could've
worked, I'd lost one of my kin
burdened, I donated the quarters
anonymously to Cub's laundry fund.

sleepover

girl talk with Swan and Poodle
"who's the cutest?"
I remain quiet -
not innocent, desperately seeking.

we lay on our bellies on pillows
snacking on sweet and salty popcorn
divulging our intimate moments

Wolf took me up in a hot air balloon
in exchange for lemon bars
questioned me about illustrious poets
clueless, we crashed

Bengal and Poodle imagined dragons
to train and places to ride them
he fell asleep
a kiss on top of her head

Elephant missed the exit to go home
because directions were not Swan's skills
generous, he asked her to drive
and let her toy with the radio knobs

would I have that hope again?

obstinate

Wolf surprised me with a corset for Halloween
"it'll add to your starlet value," he tempted
I let him dress me
but gentleness was not included in his courtesy
holding my wrists back, he pulled the laces tight
too tight - I asked to breathe
he did not hear me
last strength, I told him it hurt
he pulled tighter; I didn't push him away
afraid of my worth diminishing further
I'm left with my skin coated in
sweet licorice and tart raspberries.

dr care

Cub would ask if I was going to bed
I'd say yes, but my eyes would say no,
no drink the same without us being chatty

cutting his hair in the bathroom sink
taking a bus ride together on a meandering path
staying up on a blacked out night

Cub made me laugh when I wanted to cry

I poured detergent for his laundry
bought chicken soup on a sick day
helped him study for math

his mere presence was my bandaid too

but healers are not meant to love their patients.

smitten

harboring:
hum of a microwave ricochets of
empty Angry Orchard bottles
crookedly lined up for paper ball bowling
framed moment:
series of failed tosses
but giggly nudges
I notice the streaks in my hair
match Cub's Vans
we're on the same wavelength
our first strike
his invitation to hang
agreeing is an island
of betrayal between us.

coveting:
salt, agave, and lime chased down by chocolate
syrup
I watched Bengal and Poodle launch into a duet
of open doors
under the honey desk light, I threw back more
shots
until I didn't want to be a third wheel.
seeking my own party, I stumbled onto Wolf's
dinghy

dancing as he steered away from the shore
I leaned in toward him, needy I was labeled
recoiling, I fell overboard
a guest who'd overstayed her welcome
Cub fished me out, my buoy, he carried me to
land
Wolf's cunning gaze told me he
deciphered the connection between Cub and I
my feeble protest interrupted by Cub, "not worth
it"
I was left wickedly surprised he took my side.

attached

true to his name
Wolf left the pack first
not even telling Cub
much to his distraught
Wolf left behind
his papa roach record
cactus ashtray
mad libs
I asked Cub if he wanted them
but in his decline, I saved them
realizing I was attached
in a way he never had been.

distracted

12:29pm: my mind skitters, a white mouse on
black tiles
Cub walks into the room his hair disheveled by
the wind
a smile that can power New York -
my mouth is dry.
our shared dictionary has its pages ripped out,
guilt thick having driven Wolf away
the only word left, "hey"
not hello - we're past formality - not hi - we're
past casualness
now we might as well have Broca's aphasia
around each other.

when Wolf said he was too conservative to be
with me
Cub consoled me, "a peridot from the galaxy."
now in the seat across, he faces others in the
room
I listen
doodle, play with my bracelet, twirl my pen
sneak glances, notice his stubble
the back slouch, the arm hugging the couch
he strums a martin, discusses existentialism,
puffs his e-cig;

catches me sharing in his jest, asks me how my
day is
my eyes drop, "okay" I murmur
2:18pm: my assignment remains untouched.

impasse

paired up science lab partners
to recreate papier-mâché Vesuvius
a chance to be more than dormmates
we committed to our project
Cub got the packaging
I had the ingredients
I explorative, him rushing
we roared in disagreements
improper measurements
the structure short-fused and unstable
our opinions lashed at jugulars
I wanted to try again, but not Cub
our high regard for each other now lopsided.

end of an age

ghost town weekend
Swan and Poodle reunited with their families
I turned to Cub for entertainment
he tossed me a black controller to
occupy myself with demolition as he checked
his phone
I rammed my zombie into a wall, aware soon
we wouldn't be sharing strawberry lemonade
moments.

Cub's mockery of my inability to play
interrupted by Bengal and Elephant walking in
I faded into the amber tapestry as they restarted
the game
the crackle of red dorito bags littering the floor
brighter than the blood against the slate clouds
on screen
I twiddled my thumbs.

a round of Svedka shots unfinished
Elephant asked me to scratch his back with a
hanger
I lost my footing
Cub's power outlet and vanilla freshener
clattered to the ground

jump, squeal in rose embarrassment
only to catch them chortling.

we were never going to get this time back
at least I could say I had this one night with my
boys

dear Cub

are you listening to sonata 29 in the basement or
me?
before you disappear again, I understand your
absence.
concern was my friend, during your sixty hour
work weeks.
doors closed, the comfort quilt of Netflix did not
help me forget my
eggshell heart cracked from your lack of
response.
forever 19, our last day, I helped you clean out,
unable to say
goodbye, a 14 page letter, preemptive strike to
your last word
home was an igloo, I missed your seal bark, you
I still love you.
July 1st: "I'm not coming back," you said, a
kid no more, you took the responsibility to
lift your family's financial burden - and shut
everyone -
me - out. I wished on shooting stars, on pennies
tossed into
Niagara falls: for you to stay a part of my life.
And then -

omnipresent clouds intermittently rained, the
down
pour began when I walked right into you, the
quintessential defining moment, a fair
Roman you weren't but rather a cold general I
stood in front of, words swallowed like
traveler's club to forget, to give courage to
ignore
until I couldn't anymore.
veal parmesan, lunch for two, offered and
accepted
we went ice-skating after; I wobbled, tipped
forward.
xenophobia flooded me, no trust in the face I
thought I knew, but
you caught me, imbalanced yourself, and down
we went the
Zoo york watch I bought you ticking forward.

cross-country

surrounded by too many memories
I picked a getaway for Poodle and I
twenty-eight hundred miles of winding roads
she was my GPS on the parkway
but she fidgeted, did our recollection align?
busy coding in fuzzy nightlight
Bengal kept warm with a kettle next to him
he'd never chosen one alliance over another.
at his door, I let Poodle go ahead
watching their delighted reunion
I hoped it sufficed to reverse my karma.

fractured

27

it was Swan who told me of his return
I laughed disbelievingly
Poodle confirmed and I embraced a scowl
Bengal and Elephant thumped down the stairs
in greeting, the girls trailed behind
as Cub climbed out of his car
I watched from my rooftop perch
letting them haul his belongings
stung he hadn't told me
we had another chance
but I didn't know how to start over.

gamble

to dispel the tension
our squad set up a match for
us jungle cats to lay it all on the field
Cub strutted and I gambled
pouncing on the ball of discussion
I'd been practicing a backhand serve
"I gave you my all and you didn't care"
agape, he withdrew and I won respect
but he'd learned from Wolf
his consolation prize emerged from the wing
acceptance from the spectators
and advice for me to surrender
him: love, me: 0

indulge

I considered running away to
the beating churns of train wheels
tethered, I let my recollection
of periwinkle laughter
be louder than my black heartbeat

when Cub wildly punched into batting bears
having guzzled too much jungle juice
I intervened before the mauling left scars
in the way, he charged at me
"you shouldn't bother."

I didn't feel the rake of his claws draw blood;
Elephant and Bengal hauled him to bed
water bottles and Advil, I made sure he lay on
his side -
Cub murmured
"I am better off without you."

I left.
I had to.

slinging on a backpack
on my way to the platform
I heard thundering paws

chasing me down.
in step - Cub regaled a tale
of drugged turpitude, an excuse
I wouldn't pardon until
Cub's sobriety begged
"I'm sorry. you're truly a good friend."

molting, I saw he wasn't a lion yet
so I returned to the watering hole.
"do you forgive me?"
"yes," I said hesitantly.

www.ingramcontent.com/pod-product-compliance
Lightning Source LLC
La Vergne TN
LVHW010948200726
843509LV00013B/2319